ILL NATURE

John McKeown

Ill Nature
published in the United Kingdom in 2022
by Mica Press

c/o Leslie Bell
47 Belle Vue Road, Wivenhoe, Colchester, Essex CO7 9LD
www.micapress.co.uk | books@micapress.co.uk
www.campanulabooks.uk | info@campanulabooks.uk

ISBN 978-1-869848-30-9

Acknowledgements

Thanks are due to the editors of the following journals in
which some of these poems have previously appeared:
Poetry Salzburg Review, The Cannon's Mouth,
The High Window, Anthropocene, Cake Magazine,
Ink, Sweat & Tears, Foxtrot Uniform, Allegro, The Crank,
Broken Wine and The Delinquent.

"The world is not a dream carved in stone, it is made of dubious stuff subject to rot."

Simone de Beauvoir

Table of Contents

page number

Coming Down

The full Moon up all night,
yellow-faced, like a light left on
at a party with all asleep,
hangs in its descent now
in the clear dawning sky, above
the knife-edge of the iced roof.
I slit the blinds, timid, an aged neighbour
to observe its restless, solitary act; preserving
faintly, all the jaundiced fire of youth.

Swifts

The swifts, winged shrapnel
with a trilling voice,
swoop and glide against
light's weakening texture.

Brassy, lovely trumpet flakes,
I wilt at attention,
leaving all the bodies to tomorrow.
This day's torn to shreds.

Night Wind

Far off the wind like giant sheets
Snapped and re-snapped smart, ironically,
Like the echo of terrible poltergeist play.

Far off, now close, the hollow voices
Of parental ghosts, buffeting the house:
What are we, whose are we, who minds us?

We drift far off, scatter; the wind
Is the noise of deeds, arrangements,
A four-square putting away, under lock and key,

In beds of earth, in the shifting sky.

Airbrushed

The something in the air
fills me with hunger,
the watching the crows hop
between their nests against the clouded sun,
the bare branches muscling
into green suits of flesh,
the lengthening light of afternoon,
my own years lengthening;
stretches of shadow increasingly
uninterrupted by anything.

Swallows on Klimentská

I pass beneath
the swallows' swift net
of sung flight tight knit
between the roofs

momentarily raised
to their height
of quick
glorious insignificance.

On the Road

Walking round the Sun
bathed in radiance,
the straight road turning.

Walking round the Sun
the ageless Sun, ageing.
Walking into dust, borne up
in a blaze of bright magnificence.

Empty Vessels

The slim wood-pigeon swooping back and forth
Above my head, building her nest
In the fresh leafed maple tree.

There are other nests along the street
Growing dim among the thickening leaves
Like hearts placed in fibrous chests

Invisibly doing the real, silent work.
While people make their fraying ends meet,
Empty vessels blown beneath.

Ill Nature

The days float away
like dead leaves
on a stream

dead leaves in Spring.
Somewhere a tree
in a trembling fit

shakes them loose, green
from its hair.
Somewhere dense, deep;

its trembling catching.

The Great British Sunday

Cloud-strafed light, and wind
beating about the bush;
a perspectived tangle of bare branches.

Cars of course, the minions
of a monotonous, parcelled-out fate,
the soundtrack of complacency.

The wind gets up, tries
to reach in to the strings of thought,
finds nothing more substantial than itself;

blows on, rifling things for miles.

Miser

Time, tight as a fist,
not a cat
unfurled in the sun.

Languid days are done,
the nails bite.
Nine lives into less than one.

Beautiful Night

A beautiful night outside
Unruffled trees silently shedding their leaves
A dying fire facing inwards.

The dark sky raised clear
The air still, things distinct; the world collected
Its gaze elsewhere.

Lights are sharp in the chill
Clear cut windows have nothing to hide
There's a certain perspective

Though I'm not included in it.
But somewhere a pressure has eased
A space left vacant.

Continental Drift

The low clouds' lugubrious drift:
Cold bellies chilling the spring
A damper on everything.
Plans, hopes, stretched out thin
Contingent, ridiculous.

Everything slowly disappearing.
These houses rubble, the city dust,
The very continent not even a memory.

Commission

Sculpt a keel
out of twilight
deck and rigging
and sails
all of blueing cloud.

So I can board it now
as it turns, darkening
into night
and never
suffer day again.

Monomania

The heart beats, beats,
Like something incredible,
A feat that can't be done
But is, repeatedly.

Hearing it is seeing the whole
Of Atlas, one compact
Tautened mass, in throbbing support
Of nothing but himself.

Near the Sea

Certain silver clouds
strung in distant tumultuous titanic lustre
along the landward horizon.

A limitless backbone washed up
on invisible tides of sky.
Backbone of what immaterial leviathan

denizen of what immaterial sea?
We drive on. Tides, celestial, mundane
disordering a limited perception.

The weave of a fine-strung anchor still
silvered in that solid mass
of disappearing cloud.

Moonflower

The Moon's light fused
so completely
with the vapour
of the deep low bank of cloud
it's a celestial flower
my vision the stalk
blooming it radiantly.

All reason falls away.
All emotion is fed
in this isolated moment.

Buttercups

Weighed down, I pass and repass;
while the buttercups, strewn across
the railed-off lawn, float
on stems so fine they're invisible
against the green of the grass.

Grim

It's grim, the day, the world,
What we do, what we've done,
What we'll do tomorrow, and the next.

While the birds are out of hand,
Singing like there's no tomorrow
In the greening thinning wood.

And now a blackbird, visible, close
Through the screen of bare branches.
His breast plump, beak a yellow crocus.

'Fine bird song...'

Fine bird song somewhere in the fine rain.
The sky one evenness of cloud.
The pale green fir an explosion of thrusting stillness.

The bird's voice now like a worm.
A note slithering fragile, querulous,
through the wreckage of a collapsed world.

Pure little remnant, precursor, survivor.
Bright nail waiting for the right wood.

Yellow Snow

Yellow snow where a dog has pissed
Around a human footprint.
A day of frozen, dirty snow, everything foregrounded,
In nauseous detail.
It's as if the sky is spent, has breathed its last
But no one has found out,
And if it has, it'll take some time.
Enough to clear the windshield of the car
And go to work, and do the shop on the way home,
And, oh, so much more.
Me, I want to break out,
With the bare, black twisted branches thrown
                              up against the window,
Go wherever the sky has gone.

Enough

The loftiness
of the stars'
intimate silence
is enough.

I look down
at the moths
around the streetlamp,
busily unthreading
the web
of every question.

Twilight

Where the streets end, the sun
wrestled down in a darkening
blue confusion of cloud,
people - automata - unnoticing.

Here and there, on houses' upper reaches
the faintest touches of gold
ghostly as breath on a mirror
in an empty room.

And, for a moment, the feel
of something trying to come
between one moment and the next.

A voiceless insistence
soft as air, on everything
being, already, perfectly here.

Me & My Younger Self

I climb the stairs wearily
he climbs within, wearily.
I slump in a chair,
he slumps too.
I wish I could smoke,
he lights his tenth cigarette.
I weigh out a drink,
he fills up the glass.
I sit and stare at the window,
he puts on Ravel.
I wonder what life is,
he's racked with sobs
by the music.
What is life but emotion
intensely lived?
I formulate the lesson,
he has no need to learn it.

Naivety

I never thought I'd live forever,
but I did think time would be
commodious enough for my dilatoriness.

How naive I was. It's my dilatoriness
which is endlessly commodious;
as if I were designed, not for time, but eternity.

Real Life

I've lost track of it,
my real life; but it's there
dying of cold, close by;
its shivers running through me.

I almost pity it;
naked, radical, a bag of bones,
knock-kneed, pregnant; its waters
breaking in the snow.

Self-Sacrifice

Drinking, I escape
the pressure of reality,
but remain
rooted to the spot.

The spot a cafe table
where red wine stands;
a rootless plant
I drain myself to replenish.

Relic

My new wrist watch has no tick,
and no numbers, only slivers.
All very apt, as we neither hear
or see time pass. It's just fingers,
attenuated as the silvered fragments
of the bones of a saint
under a smooth perfection of glass.

Which can neither rub my life
back into shape, or erase
one tiny period of all the waste
I unfalteringly accumulate.

Tête-à-Tête

I remember the octopus
in the undersized glass case
in the aquarium in Madrid,
so close to the sea.

The octopus: a roving animal
full of curiosity,
with a large brain.
Apparent to me, at least,

as I stood, close to the glass,
transfixed,
in a more diffuse predicament.

Past

Every moment past
free from this exists
detached in bliss.

In pain I caress each
rounded impenetrability,
like a rosary, disordered

broken on the thread of time.

Guillotine

The star's glide across the window
Cuts my throat where I sit.
It moves quick; it takes years;
Egged on by the surrounding stars,
And a little of everything that exists.

At the Hairdresser

Like a corpse the thing
sat with a black sheet
up to the neck, having
its hair cut, not me.

Avoid the eyes as you would
of a corpse, naturally,
but you're drawn magnetically,
as if by ultimate meaning.
Though all you see is gross
similarity;

all the fine shades of you,
penumbral peacock, reduced
to a life-size puppet
stuck in a chair, its strings cut.

Proof

What could be
more beautiful
than the blue dome
beneath which
we breed our horror?

Who could come up
with such
a perfect antithesis
to what we are
than a God
sick to perfection?

Order

The tramp hitches his pants
Where the diners dine,
Patting fat wallets at the tables
Under the night-bearing trees.

Trees leeching light from a sky
Aged so fine, so fragile,
It's about to break, shatter everything.
The waiters serve, the diners eat,

And the tramp, his pants tight,
Shuffles on out of the square.

Pravda

Brick, beneath all these ornate facades,
Brick piled on brick,
As bone's wed to bone beneath the skin.

You notice it here and there,
But one patch of exposure's enough
To see it everywhere.

Worn brick under crumbling stucco
As the putti flounce, the cornucopiae spill
The injunction not to be fooled.

Among the Gods

I

'When the barbarians
leave the temple, is the temple
no more a temple?'

'Less, perhaps. But the gods
to which it's dedicated
would not be gods

if they could be
so easily overrun.
Your cup is empty,

here's the jug again,
full, old friend,
drink.'

II

The loud, ungainly, unkempt,
ill-mannered barbarians gone;
sunlight streaming golden
among the quiet pillars again.

And I don't know
which gods to thank,
so I thank them all, on my knees,
clutching tight my wine-cup.

III

You smashed me in the face,
but it's you I place, broken,
among my memorials of goddesses.

Where I can play my fingers
over your jagged edges, filling in
all the missing parts.

Broken myself, of course, but
by erecting you thus, I make myself
a kind of thwarted god.

Palladia

All pale skin, pale,
Blonde-hair, sun-lit
As she strides,
Matching the pale green
Of the building.

The girls of Prague,
Matchless anywhere,
Cool in the sun, cool
In the cold; thermostatic,
Irreproachable.

Bibliophile

Against the red background
Of the passport photo
The black blazon of your hair.
And within it, the spots
Of your blue eyes, in your white skin,
Like the wings of a butterfly,
Bore into me.

I cracked the old paperback,
And there you were, your youth,
Your beauty, your personality,
A pressed flower, flushed with colour,
Retaining its life on an uncut stem.

How could I not have loved you?
How could I not have done everything to keep you?
What has withered in the nest
Of all the reasons that made
Such painful sense, that were real - then?

Now, there's just you, pert, erect,
Unfazed, undimmed, unanswerable;
Vivid, vital against the browned spine
Of a book I treasured more than you.

Open Love Letter

I'm ready for love now,
now that I'm falling apart,
now that it's hard to find
a centre where resistance can collect.

I'm ready for love now,
now that the handful who loved me have gone;
more ready than I've ever been,
as I clutch at this, now that, passing impossibility.

Bookcases

By this time next year the bookcases
will be disassembled; and if
they can be put back together
they'll be elsewhere. Not with me,
with her, wherever she is;
the books will be with me,
my books, or in boxes waiting
while I save to house them
in my new flat, the new flat
I didn't rent this year.
But next year, finally,
I'll have undone the last screw,
taken off the top and base,
slid out the shelves, removed the sides,
broken up this life.

Peekaboo

She looks into my eyes
as we pass, unsmilingly.

She looks into me
as if my skull were glass
my writhing thoughts plainly visible.

Motionless, opaque, inscrutable,
she passes, her eyes, hazel, mild,
clear as untroubled, standing water.

'About 5' 4", very slim, long dark hair'

Love has a body, has moved
in next door. I hear her opening
and closing drawers, cupboards,
wardrobes, like a detective
searching for the culprit.

Time passes with the tread of her silence,
coming in and out, the brandishing
of cutlery, the squeak of a bed.

And each night is full of the pressure of it,
against the wall, spreading through the floor,
over the roof, and on into the dark
and another empty dawn.

Old Get

The older I get the more
Astonishing they become:
The fresh, supple, graceful girls,
Various and colourful as flowers.

I become old as stone, as grey,
But lacking stone's indifference, solidity.
Each fresh beauty cuts me to the bone;
Gutting me of acceptance of being alone.

Haunted Orchid
for Lina

If an orchid were haunted
it would be like you:
shiveringly delicate
tenaciously fragile.

But I'd have no green-fingered priest
called in to conduct
some botanical exorcism. No, I'd keep you
under observation,

under glass, the sweep of glass
sealed around me.

After Reading Cavafy

While the mock candle
made to flicker like flame
glows deep autumn yellow,

and the blinds are strips
of shadow waiting to be parted
unsupported on the wall,

come to me, shade of you,
slip into my bed, slip
your lovely sliver of flesh.

Come to me, really, shade
of memory, be, once more
the lovely flesh that loved me.

Forgotten

There's not one look
in your eyes, one grimace,
one grin, one hint
of a smile, one twitch
or shift of your figure
I can keep.
          The gathered
body of you is lifted
from my hands, floated out
into the stream, while I sit
on the bare bank,
fragmented as Ophelia.

Clepsydra

Stoney-faced on the street,
Politely ignorant at best;
The girl next door's voice fills
The toilet as I have a piss.

Soft as an angel she is,
Singing, invisible, ethereal…
I hold this part of her tight,
Listen: a lilting swell of golden light.

(*A Clepsydra was an ancient instrument used to measure
time by the dropping of water from a graduated vessel
through a small opening….14th/15th century Latin, from
Greek Klepsudra: to steal water.*)

Wishbone

As I pass her it's her breastbone I note
moving softly beneath the pale skin.
In that instant she is the perfect mould
into which I could pour every damned reserve.

And I fancy she knows it,
and something passes between us.
There's a snap as of a wishbone,
a fusion, a recognition;

as our bodies pull quickly apart.

Togetherness

You're an egg
asleep
my spoiled
my rotten love.

While I hatch
broodily
in your
blessed silence

sun after
little sun
divorced
from the light.

To a Hedge-Witch

Tiny tornadoes of green
Bursting silently from the trees
And birdsong pinpricks of light
In the warming motion of the air.

And as I sit, pink blossoms thick
Bid for tender of my fingertips.
To touch the softness of your lips
The glistening root your body is.

The Gold Standard

All this time
while you've been
moving on,
I've remained
the one possessor
of your true value.

Locked in a vault
whose combination I've lost,
lie, numbered, the still moist
petals of your smile.

Branded

You can't know
the peck of your kiss
is a branding iron.
Or that for all
my sour talk
I'm just a calf who needs
the sweet milk
of his own small horizon.

You can't know.
But how that ignorance
burns.

The Chinese Lady Serves the Wine

Everything
like a spilling bolt of silk
and thought embroidery
the mind may or may not stitch.

Nothing matters
for everything
is the blue silk
or the gold silk
or the watered silk
of Heaven.

Moving On

Only movement
makes things bearable,
hell in a handcart
but the wheels are turning.

Only movement;
that's why I check the sky
as you maunder on,
speech a bubble of death
at your lips;
but that low star
is in a different place.

Pianissimo
for Helen

She appears, conjured
By the soft piano notes
The silk lament of horn
Afloat out of the café.

She sits down there
Pale hair, pale skin, distinct
Against the black leatherette
The white brick wall.

All the pain, trouble, torment
A gentle magic in her eyes
At rest in me
Restless outside,

With morning coffee
Under the maple trees.

CPSIA information can be obtained
at www.ICGtesting.com
Printed in the USA
LVHW110940220922
728951LV00005B/280